SOUTHGATE

RULES

Hi, pleased to meet you.

We hope you enjoy our book about Gareth Southgate!

I'm **VARbot** with all the facts and stats!

SIMON DAN

W
WELBECK

VAR

THIS IS A WELBECK CHILDREN'S BOOK
Published in 2021 by Welbeck Children's Books Limited
An imprint of the Welbeck Publishing Group
20 Mortimer Street, London W1T 3JW
Text © 2021 Simon Mugford
Design & Illustration © 2021 Dan Green
ISBN: 978-1-78312-857-0

Writer: Simon Mugford
Designer and Illustrator: Dan Green
Design manager: Sam James
Executive editor: Suhel Ahmed
Production: Arlene Alexander

A catalogue record for this book is available from the British Library.

Printed in the UK
10 9 8 7 6 5 4 3 2 1

Statistics and records correct as of September 2021

FOOTBALL SUPERSTARS

SOUTHGATE

RULES

SIMON MUGFORD   DAN GREEN

CONTENTS

CHAPTER 1

SOUTHGATE, YOU'RE THE ONE

SOUTHGATE, YOU'RE THE ONE!

Gareth Southgate is the most successful England manager in more than 50 years. His

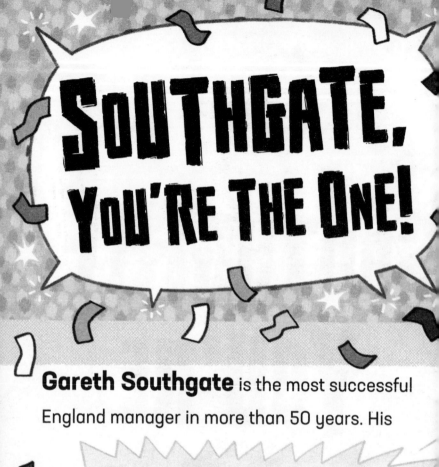

INSPIRATIONAL LEADERSHIP

and calm, quiet personality have won him respect and admiration that goes beyond football.

THIS BOOK IS ALL ABOUT **HIM!**

WHAT MAKES **GARETH** GREAT?

Leadership
Gareth always takes responsibility for his decisions, even when things go wrong.

Caring
He has time for everyone in the squad and staff, from star players to the coach driver.

People person
Gareth gets the best out of everyone he works with.

Intelligence
He knows that football is about much more than kicking a ball.

Strength
Gareth is seen as 'Mr Nice', but he is tough when it's time to make a hard decision.

SOUTHGATE
IS ONE OF THE BEST
IN THE BUSINESS!

SOUTHGATE IN NUMBERS

More than **600** career appearances as a club player.

57 ... England caps

2 ... Football League Cup wins

1 ... Football League First Division (now the Championship) win

39 ... wins as England manager

1 OBE
(order of the British Empire - awarded by the Queen)

ONE IS ROYALLY IMPRESSED!

3 ... semi-finals and

1 final as England manager

Plus, he's a hero to

MILLIONS

of England fans!

SOUTHGATE I.D.

NAME: *Gareth Southgate*

DATE OF BIRTH: *3 September 1970*

PLACE OF BIRTH: *Watford, England*

HEIGHT: *1.83 metres*

POSITIONS: *Defender, midfielder, manager*

CLUBS: *Crystal Palace, Aston Villa, Middlesbrough*

NATIONAL TEAM: *England*

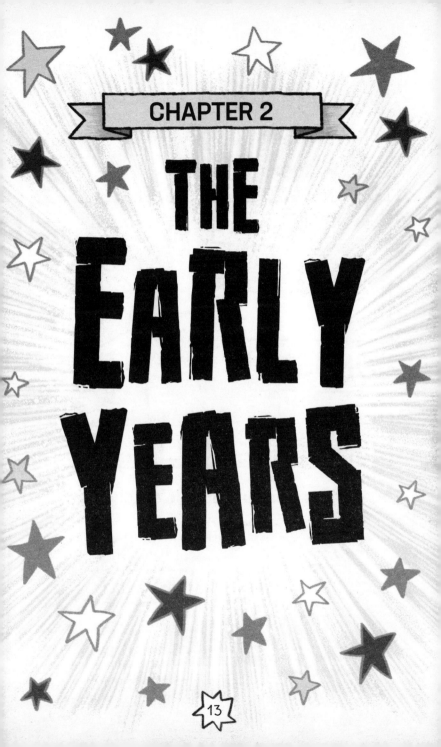

CHAPTER 2

THE EARLY YEARS

Gareth Southgate was born in **Watford** in **1970** and grew up in **Crawley** in **West Sussex**.

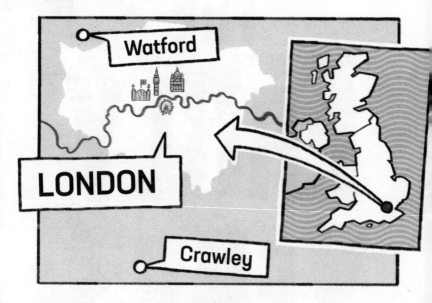

Gareth was a brilliant athlete at school and the **TRIPLE JUMP** county champion!

He played rugby, cricket and basketball, but his big love was . . . **FOOTBALL.**
He played at school, after school, at the weekends and trained with **Southampton.**

Southampton let him go when he was **13,** but the disappointment made Gareth even more determined to succeed.

Gareth worked hard at school and did well in his exams. He even thought about becoming a **journalist**.

But there was **ALWAYS** football. At 15, he was training with south London club **Crystal Palace**.

They offered him an apprenticeship - he was being **PAID** to play football. **WOW!**

The boys at **Crystal Palace** were tough. To them, Gareth was the 'posh' kid with goofy teeth and a big nose. They gave him a **hard time.**

But Gareth was tough, too. He won his team-mates over with his **football skills** and **smart talking**.

He became **captain** of the youth team and learned to be a **leader**.

Chris Powell was in the youth team with Gareth at Palace.

Now he is Southgate's assistant coach with **England!**

"GARETH KNOWS HE CAN TRUST ME BECAUSE WE GO BACK SO FAR."

CHAPTER 3

ON THE PITCH

Gareth made his first-team debut for **Crystal Palace** in **1991** – away to Liverpool in the old **First Division** (Palace lost 3-0).

Gareth became the **team captain** when he was only **22!**

Palace were **relegated** from the newly created Premier League in 1992-93, but they bounced straight back up again the following season as **First Division champions.**

Gareth scored **NINE** league goals in Palace's **title-winning** season in **1993-94.**

In 1995, Gareth left Palace to join **Aston Villa** where he switched from playing in **midfield** to **centre-back**.

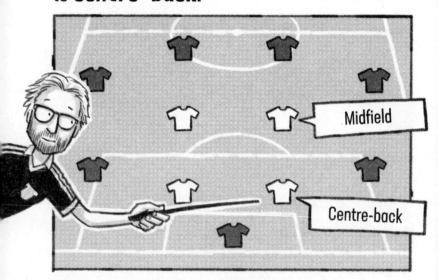

Midfield

Centre-back

His first game was against the mighty **Manchester United.** Villa won 3-1!

24

Gareth won the

League Cup

in his first season at Villa.

He made more than 240 appearances for Villa, helped them qualify for the **UEFA Cup** in 1995-96 and reached the 1999-2000 **FA Cup final.**

In July 2001, after **six seasons** at Aston Villa, Gareth joined **Middlesbrough** for £6.5 million (about £25 million today).

As the **club captain,** he led Boro to a **League Cup** win in 2004.

This was Middlesbrough's **FIRST EVER** trophy.

Gareth's last game as a player was the **2006 UEFA Cup Final** – it was a fantastic achievement for Middlesbrough, even though they were eventual runners-up to **Sevilla.**

Shortly after joining Aston Villa in 1995,
England manager **Terry Venables** handed
Gareth his England debut in a friendly
against **Portugal.**

DO YOUR COUNTRY PROUD.

It was an **incredible honour.**
Gareth's life with the national
team had begun . . .

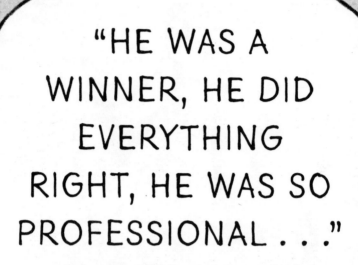

"HE WAS A WINNER, HE DID EVERYTHING RIGHT, HE WAS SO PROFESSIONAL . . ."

Steve McClaren, Southgate's manager at Middlesbrough

CHAPTER 4

IT'S COMING HOME

EURO 96

EURO 96

31

EURO 96 was the first international football tournament to be held in England for **30 YEARS.**

As the host nation, England played all their games at **Wembley.**

The old Wembley stadium

The last one was the *World Cup in 1966* ... which *England won!*

Really? No one ever mentions that.

ENGLAND 1966!

SPORT NEWS WE WON! YAAY!

The whole country was **very excited.**

There was even a song about it that you may

have heard . . .

Gareth was part of an **AWESOME** England squad in 1996. Top team-mates included . . .

Tony Adams
The inspirational Arsenal man was the centre-back and captain.

Paul Ince
Midfield master was known as 'The Guv'nor'.

Stuart Pearce
The tough-as-nails defender was nicknamed 'Psycho'.

Pearce missed a **penalty** at the **1990 World Cup**.

THANKS FOR THE REMINDER!

David Seaman
The goalkeeper was famous for his moustache and brightly coloured strip!

COOL LOOK!

Teddy Sheringham
The Spurs and Man United legend was a goalscoring machine.

Alan Shearer
Fantastic striker who would become the Premier League's record scorer with 260 goals.

36

Paul Gascoigne
'Gazza' was a uniquely gifted midfielder capable of both magic and mayhem!

Gazza famously cried in the 1990 World Cup semi-final.

The manager, **Terry Venables** had won **La Liga** as **Barcelona** head coach and took **Tottenham** to their **FA Cup win** in 1991.

England's first game, against **Switzerland** ended in a 1-1 draw. But next came the **BIG ONE** . . . England vs **Scotland.**

Alan Shearer put England ahead early in the second half, but then Scotland had a penalty . . .

. . . which was **SAVED** by David Seaman!

POW!

A minute later the ball was at the other end. **Paul Gascoigne** flicked the ball over defender Colin Hendry and volleyed it home to score one of the **best England goals ever**.

BAM!

England-Scotland is the **oldest fixture** in **international football**. They played their first match in **1872!**

The **final group match** was against a very strong **Netherlands** team. It was Gareth's job to stop Arsenal legend **Dennis Bergkamp** scoring.

And he did!

Shearer and Sheringham scored **TWO goals** each as the Dutch were thrashed **4-1**.

England faced **Spain** in the quarter-final.
A tight game ended **0-0** and went to the
dreaded **penalty shoot-out.**

But Spain **missed a penalty** and Seaman
saved another - England were through!

ENG-GER-LAND! IT'S COMING HOME!

IT'S VIRTUAL
INSANITY!

ENGLAND

41

26 JUNE 1996

EURO 96 SEMI-FINAL

GERMANY 1-1 ENGLAND (7-6 ON PENALTIES)

It was the biggest game at Wembley for years! **Alan Shearer** put England ahead after just **THREE** minutes, but it was **1–1** as the game went to **extra-time.**

Paul Gascoigne came so close to winning it for England - **NOOO** - so it was **penalties again.**

OH NO!

The England manager asked the team who would take the **sixth penalty** . . . and **Gareth** put his hand up.

He took his **shot** . . .

URGH!

But HIS penalty was **saved** . . .

I CAN'T BELIEVE IT'S ALL OVER.

IT IS NOW!

NO!

Gareth played **every minute** of **all England's games** at EURO 96.

75,000 fans at Wembley and **MILLIONS** watching on TV saw Gareth in tears, as his team-mates and manager gathered around him.

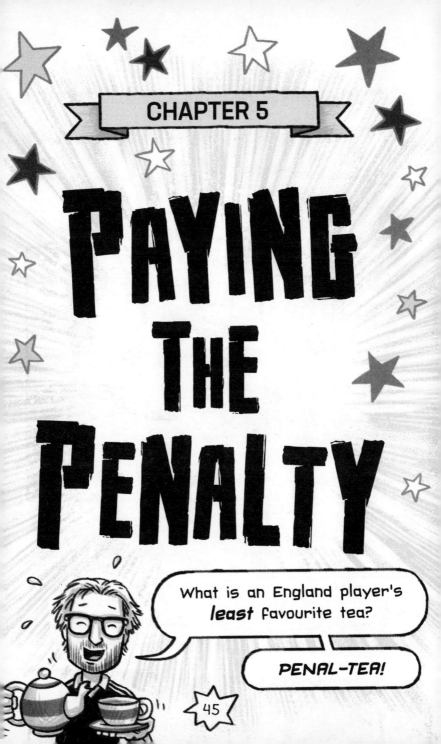

CHAPTER 5

PAYING THE PENALTY

What is an England player's *least* favourite tea?

PENAL-TEA!

The penalty miss made Gareth **world famous overnight.** It was all over the TV, in the papers.

Gareth couldn't **escape** from it, even when he went on holiday thousands of miles away in **Bali.**

But Gareth received **support** from people all over the country. Everyone from **politicians** to **pop stars** tried to make him **feel better**.

Gareth even managed to laugh about it. He was in a Pizza Hut advert with **Stuart Pearce** and **Chris Waddle,** who had missed penalties at the 1990 World Cup semi-final.

PENALTY 101

Gareth's penalty was a bad one, no question. But how do you take a good penalty?

- **Stay calm and focus.**

- **Ignore everything and everyone, especially the keeper.**

- **Decide which way to hit the ball and stick to it.**

DO NOT KICK IT HARD AND HOPE!

BLAM!

Most penalties are scored in the **bottom-left corner**.

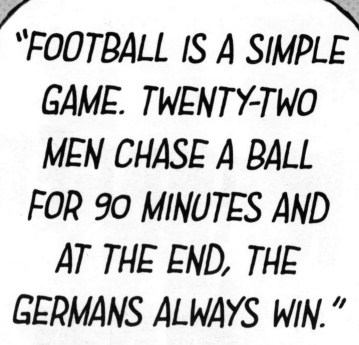

"FOOTBALL IS A SIMPLE GAME. TWENTY-TWO MEN CHASE A BALL FOR 90 MINUTES AND AT THE END, THE GERMANS ALWAYS WIN."

Gary Lineker (Former England striker and current Match of the Day presenter.)

After **five seasons** as a player at Middlesbrough, Gareth became **the manager** in the summer of **2006.**

He brought in new players and scored some big wins against **Chelsea, Arsenal** and a massive **8-1 victory** over **Manchester City.**

City were managed by ex-England manager **Sven Göran-Eriksson**

Middlesbrough were relegated in **May 2009** and Gareth was **sacked** in October that year, during his **fourth season** in charge.

"IT WAS THE FAILURE THAT . . . TAUGHT ME WHERE I NEEDED TO IMPROVE . . . AND . . . LED TO ME MANAGING THE ENGLAND TEAM"

Gareth learnt **A LOT** managing Middlesbrough.

He was a team-mate . . . and then he became
the **BOSS.** Not all the players liked that.

But Gareth soon gained their **trust.**

He was firm but fair, supportive,

encouraging and reasonable.

He learned from the disappointments

of **relegation** and being

sacked and **came**

back stronger.

Just like he did after

the penalty miss.

In **2021,** the city of **Middlesbrough** awarded Gareth the **'Freedom of the City'** - an honour that recognised what a great leader he is on and off the pitch.

CHAPTER 7

THE ENGLAND MAN

In **2013,** four years after leaving Middlesbrough, Gareth became the **manager** of the **England under–21s.**

Based at the brand new **St George's Park National Football Centre,** Gareth would help develop a new generation of England players.

Harry Kane, **Jack Grealish** and **Marcus Rashford** are just some of the players Gareth managed in the under-21s.

KANE

GREALISH

RASHFORD

At **EURO 2016**, England were *terrible*.
They scraped through the group stage and
then . . . were knocked out of the tournament
by **ICELAND.**

Iceland were
ranked 36th in
the world.

Manager Roy Hodgson resigned

immediately after the game.

I HOPE YOU'LL SEE AN
ENGLAND TEAM IN A
FINAL SOON.

63

Sam Allardyce was given the job, but left after only **ONE game** in charge. It was another low point for England.

OH, OOPS!

FA RULES

So our man Gareth stepped in - as **temporary coach** for four games. England had World Cup qualifiers to play, including one against Scotland.

England won **3−0** and in November 2016 he was **given the job.**

One of the first things Gareth did was to **drop the captain** – England's all-time top goalscorer **Wayne Rooney.**

It was a big moment. Gareth was building a **new team.** The Southgate era had begun.

"I'M DETERMINED TO GIVE THE COUNTRY A TEAM THAT THEY'RE PROUD OF."

Gareth Southgate, 2016

CHAPTER 8

RUSSIAN ADVENTURE

England topped their group to qualify for the **2018 World Cup,** but . . . Gareth was still building his **young team.** Hopes of a successful tournament in Russia were not high.

"THE QUARTER-FINALS SHOULD BE THE TARGET."

"WE'LL DO WELL TO GET OUT OF THE GROUP."

England's opening game was against **Tunisia.** The new captain **Harry Kane** put England ahead early on, only for Tunisia to **equalise** through a penalty.

'Same old England' thought the fans . . . except Kane was there to head home a **winner** in stoppage time.

Against **Panama,** England were unstoppable. **SIX goals,** including a **hat-trick** from Kane, gave them the country's **best ever start** in the World Cup.

POW!

That **6-1** win over Panama is England's **biggest ever** World Cup victory.

3 JULY 2018

WORLD CUP 2016 ROUND OF 16

ENGLAND 1-1 COLOMBIA (4-3 ON PENALTIES)

England went ahead but Colombia equalised in stoppage time. **NOOOO!**

The fans went through the agony of **extra-time,** then the dreaded **penalty shoot-out** . . .

OH NO, NOT AGAIN!

GULP!

. . . which **England WON!** It was incredible – Southgate had led England to their **first ever** shoot-out win in the World Cup.

While England were celebrating, Southgate consoled **Mateus Uribe,** the Colombia player who missed his penalty.

England faced **Sweden** in the **quarter-final.** They had **NEVER** beaten Sweden at the World Cup . . . but goals from **Harry Maguire** and **Dele Alli** changed that!

Against expectations, England were in the **World Cup semi-final** for the first time since 1990.

WOW!

But despite **Kieran Trippier's** early wonder goal, England were beaten by Croatia and the midfield magic of **Luka Modrić.**

England were out of the World Cup. But something was **different** about **_THIS_** England exit.

Southgate's England was **different**. The players **worked** for each other **as a team**. They were young, funny and likeable.

AND THEY RODE **INFLATABLE UNICORNS** IN A SWIMMING POOL!

Gareth Southgate was fast becoming a **NATIONAL TREASURE,** a hero in a **waistcoat,** who finally gave England fans something to **smile about.**

Southgate station in London renamed itself for two days in his honour.

"THESE GUYS HAD AN OPPORTUNITY TO START FROM SCRATCH AND CREATE THEIR OWN HISTORY. THAT'S WHAT WE ARE FOCUSED ON."

Gareth Southgate

CHAPTER 9

BIG BOSSES

Being the England manager is a **tough job.**

The national team are only together for a few weeks each year. It takes a **special person** to **unite a team** in a short time and do well in a tournament.

Do well and you are hero, a **NATIONAL ICON.** Lose and you might want to go and **hide away.**

SIR ALF RAMSEY

YEARS MANAGED: **1962-1974**

BEST RESULT: **1966 World Cup winner**

As the only manager to bring home a major tournament trophy - the **1966 World Cup** - **Sir Alf Ramsey** is the manager with the record to beat.

England beating **West Germany 4–2** after extra time at **Wembley** is the stuff of football legend.

Geoff Hurst is **STILL** the only player to score a **hat-trick** in a **World Cup final**.

Sir Alf managed the *mighty Ipswich Town* before England!

Ed Sheeran, Ipswich Town fan

IPSWICH F.C.

COOL!

SIR BOBBY ROBSON

YEARS MANAGED: **1982-1990**

BEST RESULT: **1990 World Cup semi-final**

Robson was in charge for the **1986 World Cup quarter-final** against **Argentina,** when **Diego Maradona** scored his **"Hand of God"** goal (he hand-balled it into the net).

Robson also took England to the **1990 World Cup semi-final.** England lost the penalty shoot-out to West Germany (of course!)

Paul Gascoigne cried.

Sir Bobby was **ALSO** an Ipswich Town manager!

PERFECT! COME ON YOU TRACTOR BOYS!

GRAHAM TAYLOR

YEARS MANAGED: **1990-1994**

BEST RESULT: **EURO 1992 group stage**

A serious football man, but failure to qualify for the 1994 World Cup brought Taylor's time to an end.

TERRY VENABLES

YEARS MANAGED: **1994-1996**

BEST RESULT: **EURO 1996 semi-final**

Gareth's manager at EURO 1996. 'El Tel' was funny, charming and very popular with the public.

GLENN HODDLE

YEARS MANAGED: **1996-1999**

BEST RESULT: **1998 World Cup round of 16**

Manager for another infamous Argentina match, in which David Beckham was sent off and another penalty shoot-out was lost.

KEVIN KEEGAN

YEARS MANAGED: **1999-2000**

BEST RESULT: **EURO 2000 group stage**

EURO 2000 was another disappointment for England fans, but Keegan's team did beat Germany!

SVEN GÖRAN-ERIKSSON

YEARS MANAGED: **2001-2006**

BEST RESULTS: **2002 World Cup, EURO 2004, 2006 World Cup quarter-finals**

England's first non-English manager took the team further than it had gone in a decade, but with players like Wayne Rooney and David Beckham he should have done better.

STEVE McCLAREN

YEARS MANAGED: **2006-2007**

BEST RESULT: **A 1-1 draw against Brazil in a friendly.**

McClaren was Gareth's gaffer at Middlesbrough, but could not find success with England, failing to qualify for EURO 2008.

FABIO CAPELLO

YEARS MANAGED: **2007-2012**

BEST RESULT: **2010 World Cup round of 16**

The Italian won lots of qualifiers and friendlies but England were poor at the 2010 World Cup and were knocked out by Germany (of course!)

ROY HODGSON

YEARS MANAGED: **2012-16**

BEST RESULT: **EURO 2012 quarter-final**

Roy is highly respected in football, but THAT Iceland game was too much.

Under Roy, England lost to Italy in a penalty shoot-out at **EURO 2012**.

TOP WINNERS

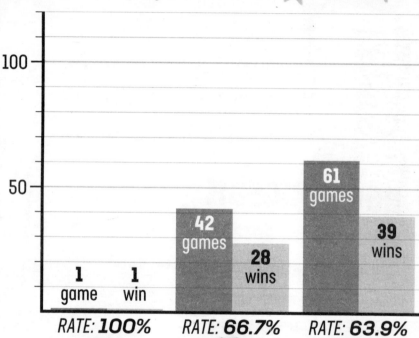

100 —

50 —

1 game   **1** win

42 games   **28** wins

61 games   **39** wins

RATE: **100%**   RATE: **66.7%**   RATE: **63.9%**

SAM ALLARDYCE   **FABIO CAPELLO**   **GARETH SOUTHGATE**

THAT'S NOT FAIR!

THESE ARE THE ENGLAND BOSSES WITH SOME OF THE BEST RECORDS OF WINNING:

113 games

69 wins

67 games

40 wins

28 games

17 wins

RATE: **61.1%**

RATE: **59.7%**

RATE: **59.7%**

SIR ALF RAMSEY

GLENN HODDLE

SVEN GÖRAN-ERIKSSON

CHAPTER 10

THE SOUTHGATE SQUAD

93

HARRY KANE

DATE OF BIRTH: **28 JULY 1993**

HEIGHT: **1.88 m**

POSITION: **CENTRE-FORWARD**

CLUB: **TOTTENHAM HOTSPUR**

STAR RATING: ★★★★★

As one of the **world's top strikers**, doubts were raised at **EURO 2020** when Kane failed to score in the group stage, but were quickly forgotten when his goals in the knock-out games took England to the final.

SOUTHGATE SAYS:

"HE'S OUR MOST IMPORTANT PLAYER, THERE'S NO DOUBT ABOUT THAT."

RAHEEM STERLING

DATE OF BIRTH:

8 DECEMBER 1994

HEIGHT: **1.70 m**

POSITION: **WINGER / FORWARD**

CLUB: **MANCHESTER CITY**

STAR RATING: ★★★★★

Terrifying defences with his **endless energy** and **speedy runs,** Sterling defied his critics to be England's best player at **EURO 2020.** The self-styled **'Boy from Brent'** is well on his way to England legend status.

SOUTHGATE SAYS:

"HE IS A FIGHTER. HE HAS INCREDIBLE RESILIENCE AND HUNGER."

MARCUS RASHFORD

DATE OF BIRTH: **31 OCTOBER 1997**

HEIGHT: **1.85 m**

POSITION: **FORWARD**

CLUB: **MANCHESTER UNITED**

STAR RATING: ★★★★

The Manchester United forward became a household name during the Coronavirus pandemic campaigning for underprivileged children. The outpouring of support after his penalty miss in the EURO 2020 final proved his status as a **National Hero.**

"YOU CAN ONLY MARVEL AT WHAT HE'S ACHIEVED . . ."

JACK GREALISH

DATE OF BIRTH: **10 SEPTEMBER 1995**

HEIGHT: **1.78 m**

POSITION: **WINGER/ATTACKING MIDFIELDER**

CLUB: **MANCHESTER CITY**

STAR RATING: ★★★★

Seen as England's most exciting **creative player,** the £100 million Man City man was involved in both goals against Germany. He has been compared to **Lionel Messi.** No pressure then Jack!

SOUTHGATE SAYS:

"WE KNOW HE IS A REALLY SPECIAL TALENT AND HE CAN HAVE A BIG IMPACT."

JADON SANCHO

DATE OF BIRTH: **25 MARCH 2000**

HEIGHT: **1.80 m**

POSITION: **WINGER**

CLUB: **MANCHESTER UNITED**

STAR RATING: ★★★

"HE HAS EXPLOSIVE POTENTIAL."

BUKAYO SAKA

DATE OF BIRTH:

5 SEPTEMBER 2001

HEIGHT: **1.78 m**

POSITION: **WINGER/LEFT-BACK/MIDFIELDER**

CLUB: **ARSENAL**

STAR RATING: ★★★

"I CAN'T SPEAK HIGHLY ENOUGH OF HIM."

MASON MOUNT

DATE OF BIRTH:

10 JANUARY 1999

HEIGHT: **1.78 m**

POSITION: **ATTACKING/CENTRAL MIDFIELDER**

CLUB: **CHELSEA**

STAR RATING: ★★★★

"HE IS AN EXCEPTIONAL PLAYER."

PHIL FODEN

DATE OF BIRTH: **28 MAY 2000**

HEIGHT: **1.71 m**

POSITION: **MIDFIELDER**

CLUB: **MANCHESTER CITY**

STAR RATING: ★★★

"HE WILL BE FABULOUS FOR ENGLAND FOR YEARS."

LUKE SHAW

DATE OF BIRTH: **12 JULY 1995**

HEIGHT: **1.85 m**

POSITION: **LEFT-BACK**

CLUB: **MANCHESTER UNITED**

STAR RATING: ★★★★

"HE'S CAPABLE OF BEING THE BEST LEFT-BACK IN THE COUNTRY."

SOUTHGATE SAYS:

KALVIN PHILLIPS

DATE OF BIRTH:

2 DECEMBER 1995

HEIGHT: **1.78 m**

POSITION: **MIDFIELDER**

CLUB: **LEEDS UNITED**

STAR RATING: ★★★★

SOUTHGATE SAYS:

"HE'S A FABULOUS CHARACTER AND A FANTASTIC ATHLETE."

DECLAN RICE

DATE OF BIRTH: **14 JANUARY 1999**

HEIGHT: **1.85 m**

POSITION:

DEFENSIVE MIDFIELDER/CENTRE-BACK

CLUB: **WEST HAM UNITED**

STAR RATING: ★★★

"HE'S A FANTASTIC PLAYER TO WORK WITH."

KIERAN TRIPPIER

DATE OF BIRTH:

19 SEPTEMBER 1990

HEIGHT: **1.73 m**

POSITION: **RIGHT-BACK**

CLUB: **ATLÉTICO MADRID**

STAR RATING: ★★★

"HE IS A DEFENSIVE ANIMAL."

JOHN STONES

DATE OF BIRTH: **28 MAY 1994**

HEIGHT: **1.88 m**

POSITION: **CENTRE-BACK**

CLUB: **MANCHESTER CITY**

STAR RATING: ★★★

"HE IS BACK TO HIS BEST FORM."

HARRY MAGUIRE

DATE OF BIRTH: **5 MARCH 1993**

HEIGHT: **1.94 m**

POSITION: **CENTRE-BACK**

CLUB: **MANCHESTER UNITED**

STAR RATING: ★★★★

"BEING CAPTAIN OF MANCHESTER UNITED HAS TAKEN HIM TO ANOTHER LEVEL."

JORDAN HENDERSON

DATE OF BIRTH: **17 JUNE 1990**

HEIGHT: **1.82 m**

POSITION: **MIDFIELDER**

CLUB: **LIVERPOOL**

STAR RATING: ★★★★

"HE'S ONE OF THE 'TRIBAL ELDERS'"

JORDAN PICKFORD

DATE OF BIRTH: **7 MARCH 1994**

HEIGHT: **1.85 m**

POSITION: **GOALKEEPER**

CLUB: **EVERTON**

STAR RATING: ★★★★

"HE HAD A REALLY OUTSTANDING TOURNAMENT."

TYRONE MINGS

DATE OF BIRTH:

13 MARCH 1993

HEIGHT: **1.96 m**

POSITION: **CENTRE-BACK**

CLUB: **ASTON VILLA**

STAR RATING: ★★★

"HE'S AN OUTSTANDING LEADER."

JUDE BELLINGHAM

DATE OF BIRTH: **29 JUNE 2003**

HEIGHT: **1.86 m**

POSITION: **MIDFIELDER**

CLUB: **BORUSSIA DORTMUND**

STAR RATING: ★★★

"JUDE IS PHENOMENAL . . . HE'S A HUGELY EXCITING PLAYER."

CHAPTER 11

IT'S COMING HOME ...AGAIN

EURO 2020

EURO 2020 was an unusual tournament. It was delayed for a year because of **Coronavirus** and played across Europe with mostly small crowds for safety reasons.

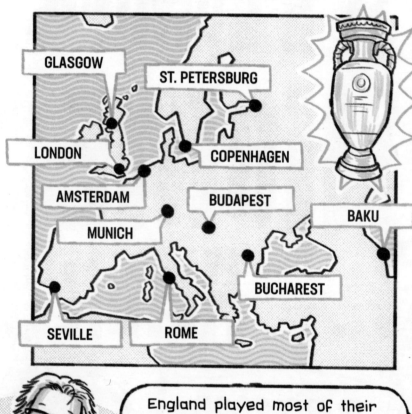

GLASGOW

ST. PETERSBURG

LONDON

COPENHAGEN

AMSTERDAM

BUDAPEST

BAKU

MUNICH

BUCHAREST

SEVILLE

ROME

England played most of their matches at *Wembley*.

It was about more than football. With a team that was **proud to play** for the country, Southgate wanted to **give the fans** something to cheer about after more than a year of lockdown.

The *excitement* was unbearable!

England's opening game was against **Croatia,** a re-match of the 2018 World Cup semi-final.

As the sun blazed down on Wembley, the young England side took control of the game, with **Kalvin Phillips** bossing the midfield.

Raheem Sterling was a constant threat - and on 57 minutes, he picked up a pass from Phillips and *BOOM* - he'd scored the **winner.**

A BRILLIANT START FOR ENGLAND.

BOFF!

"THE WIN IS IMPORTANT . . . BUT IT DOESN'T MEAN WE'VE QUALIFIED."

Next up, **Scotland,** the two old rivals were playing each other in a tournament for the first time since **1996.**

Scotland were the better team and England were lucky to get away with a **0–0 draw.** But still, it was a **clean sheet.**

Against the Czechs, **Jack Grealish** and 19-year-old **Bukayo Saka** stole the show as **Raheem Sterling** scored his second match winner of the tournament - **job done!**

"ALL THEY CAN DO AS PLAYERS IS WIN THE GROUP, WHICH THEY HAVE."

40,000 fans were allowed at Wembley to see England play **Germany** in the round of 16. **WOW!** It was a tense, nervous game but ultimately England were . . . **BRILLIANT.**

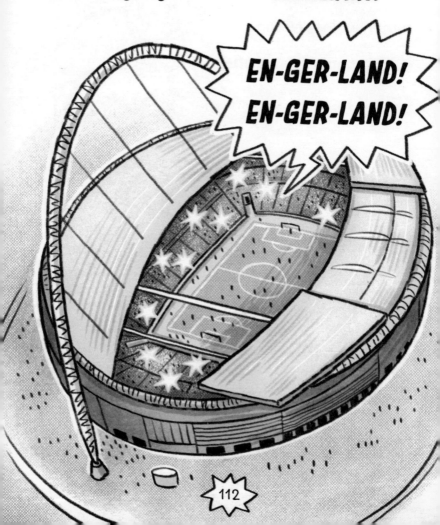

Sterling scored again and **Kane** got on the scoresheet. England had **FINALLY** knocked Germany out of a major tournament. **Wembley was roaring** with relief.

Southgate **celebrated** hard – the memory of his 1996 penalty miss all but forgotten.

"WE HAVE GIVEN PEOPLE ANOTHER DAY TO REMEMBER."

England flew to Rome for the **quarter-final** match against **Ukraine** - and kept on flying as **Harry Kane** (twice), **Harry Maguire** and **Jordan Henderson** were all on target as England won **4-0.**

BOP!

UNBELIEVABLE!

The **SEMI-FINAL** was against **Denmark.**
An incredibly tense match was **1–1** in extra-
time when England's Kane had a penalty
saved, only for him to **score** on the rebound.

Wembley went wild as Southgate took
England to their **first final** since **1966.**

"I'M SO **PROUD** OF THE PLAYERS. IT'S AN INCREDIBLE OCCASION TO BE A PART OF."

This was it. The moment England had been waiting for – **THE FINAL.** Wembley was full and the atmosphere was at fever pitch.

England were in **DREAMLAND** after **Luke Shaw** scored after just **TWO MINUTES!**

But Italy drew level, meaning extra-time and worse – the penalty shoot-out. **Pickford** saved twice, but **Marcus Rashford** missed and the giant Italian keeper **Donnarumma** saved **Jadon Sancho** and **Bukayo Saka's** efforts.

England's summer adventure was over.

YOU'RE NOT ALONE. YOU **WILL** COME BACK FROM THIS.

Beaten, but proud, Gareth Southgate stood by his players, especially the young trio of **Rashford, Sancho** and **Saka.**

After all, nobody knew better than Southgate what it meant to miss a penalty.

There was disappointment at losing the final, but Southgate has given England fans **hope** with his **young, talented squad.**

A **TROPHY** CAN'T BE FAR AWAY, CAN IT?

CHAPTER 12

SOUTHGATE RULES

SOUTHGATE RULES

1. LED ENGLAND TO THE EURO 2020 FINAL

2. SUPPORTED HIS PLAYERS IN THEIR STAND AGAINST RACISM

3. MADE A NATION HAPPY AFTER THE CORONAVIRUS PANDEMIC

4. BEAT GERMANY IN A MAJOR TOURNAMENT

5. GAVE FANS HOPE FOR THE FUTURE

QUIZ TIME!

How much do you know about GARETH SOUTHGATE? Try this quiz to find out, then test your friends!

1. At which club did Gareth start his professional career?

---

2. How many times did Gareth win the Football League Cup?

---

3. Which club did Gareth play for and manage?

---

4. Who was the England manager at EURO 96?

---

5. What did Gareth advertise after his penalty miss?

---

6. Who did Gareth replace as England manager?

---

7. Which team did England win a penalty shoot-out against in 2018?

---

8. Which England player won the Golden Boot at the 2018 World Cup?

---

9. Which team did England beat 4-0 at EURO 2020?

---

10. How many penalties did Jordan Pickford save in the EURO 2020 final?

The answers are on the next page *but no peeking!*

ANSWERS

1. Crystal Palace
2. Twice
3. Middlesbrough
4. Terry Venables
5. Pizza
6. Sam Allardyce
7. Colombia
8. Harry Kane
9. Ukraine
10. Two

SOUTHGATE:
WORDS YOU NEED TO KNOW

First Division
The top English league until the Premier League began in 1992-93.

UEFA Cup
European club competition, now replaced by the Europa League.

Premier League
The top football league in England.

St George's Park
The home of the National Football Centre, the base for all England teams.

FA Cup
The top English knockout cup competition.

League Cup
The second English knockout cup competition.

ABOUT THE AUTHORS

Simon's first job was at the Science Museum, making paper aeroplanes and blowing bubbles big enough for your dad to stand in. Since then he's written all sorts of books about the stuff he likes, from dinosaurs and rockets, to llamas, loud music and of course, football. Simon has supported Ipswich Town since they won the FA Cup in 1978 (it's true - look it up) and once sat next to Rio Ferdinand on a train. He lives in Kent with his wife and daughter, a dog, cat and two tortoises.

Dan has drawn silly pictures since he could hold a crayon. Then he grew up and started making books about stuff like trucks, space, people's jobs, *Doctor Who* and *Star Wars*. Dan remembers Ipswich Town winning the FA Cup but he

didn't watch it because he was too busy making a Viking ship out of brown paper. As a result, he knows more about Vikings than football. Dan lives in Suffolk with his wife, son, daughter and a dog that takes him for very long walks.